TOP TIPS: WELCOMING CHILDREN OF OTHER FAITHS

Gill Marchant and Andrew Smith

Copyright © 2007
First published 2007
ISBN 978 184427 250 8

Scripture Union England and Wales
207–209 Queensway, Bletchley,
Milton Keynes, MK2 2EB, England
Email:info@scriptureunion.org.uk
Website: www.scriptureunion.org.uk

Scripture Union Australia
Locked Bag 2, Central Coast Business Centre, NSW 2252
Website: www.scriptureunion.org.au

Scripture Union USA
PO Box 987, Valley Forge, PA 19482
Website: www.scriptureunion.org

All rights reserved. No part of this publication may be reproduced, stored in a retrieval system, or transmitted in any form or by any means, electronic, mechanical, photocopying, recording or otherwise, without the prior permission of Scripture Union.

Scripture quotations are taken from the HOLY BIBLE, NEW INTERNATIONAL VERSION, (NIV), © 1973, 1978, 1984 by International Bible Society. Used by permission of Hodder & Stoughton, a division of Hodder Headline Ltd. All rights reserved.

The right of Gill Marchant and Andrew Smith to be identified as authors of this work has been asserted by them in accordance with the Copyright, Designs and Patents Act 1988.

British Library Cataloguing-in-Publication Data: a catalogue record of this book is available from the British Library.

Printed and bound in Dorchester, England, by Henry Ling.

Logo, cover design, internal design: www.splash-design.co.uk
Internal illustrations: Colin Smithson
DTP layout: Richard Jefferson

Scripture Union is an international Christian charity working with churches in more than 130 countries, providing resources to bring the good news about Jesus Christ to children, young people and families and to encourage them to develop spiritually through the Bible and prayer.

As well as our network of volunteers, staff and associates who run holidays, church-based events and school Christian groups, we produce a wide range of publications and support those who use our resources through training programmes.

INTRODUCTION

What exactly is it you want to know about relating to people of other faiths? Are you concerned about whether people of other faiths can get to heaven? Do you want to know how you can most effectively share your faith with a neighbour or a colleague, a parent or a child in the school playground who comes from a faith background different from your own? Are you a church leader who is aware of the many contacts members of your church have with those from other faiths? Are you struggling with the practicalities of living out your faith in an increasingly multicultural society? And what has the Bible got to say about it?

These are complex and significant questions and Christians have used the Bible to arrive at very different conclusions. People may actually be looking for different answers and may hold varying attitudes towards the authority of scripture. Take this for example. When thinking about whether people of other faiths will be in heaven there are three traditional standpoints:

- Exclusivism affirms the uniqueness of Christ and asserts that it is only by explicit faith in him that anyone can be saved.
- Inclusivism affirms the uniqueness of Christ but includes the possibility that the death of Christ has been the means of salvation for those who do not specifically believe in him.
- Pluralism affirms God's love for all his creation and sees different religions as different (and equally valid) ways of responding to that love.

These questions are important, and there is a glossary of recommended books so you can find out more, for there is a limit to what we can cover in a book this size!

However we need to avoid getting sidetracked into seeing the people we know, including children and young people, as scalps to win or as abstract theological problems rather than individuals with whom we can have a relationship.

It is also worth noting that it is in only a few places that the Bible addresses questions relating to other faiths. It was not a significant issue for most original readers. However, there is teaching about how God's people down through the ages have (or should have) lived among people of other faiths and continued to stand out as God's people.

> **Think about...**
> What questions have motivated your interest in ministry with children of other faiths? Be honest! Write down the assumptions or beliefs you hold as you start to read this book.

WHAT THE BIBLE SAYS ABOUT LIVING AMONG PEOPLE OF OTHER FAITHS

In John 14:6, Jesus states categorically that he is the way, the truth and the life. No one can come to the Father except through him. This verse proclaims the truth about Jesus and his uniqueness as the way of salvation. These are profound truths that form the basis of our faith. But let's ask some more searching questions: who was Jesus talking to and how were they feeling at the time? What was the rest of the conversation about? What was Jesus trying to tell his friends?

Jesus' disciples were feeling uncertain and frightened about the future. They weren't engaging in a philosophical discussion about who would or would not come to God. Put in its wider context, John 14:6 doesn't tell us how we should treat people of other faiths or how we might enable them to come to faith in Jesus.

For most of the centuries covered by the Bible, God's people lived in what we would now call multi-faith or multicultural societies – living in Egypt or exiled into Babylon, or

> **Think about...**
> Think of Bible passages that relate to your work with children of other faiths; for example, Leviticus 19:9–10,33–34; Deuteronomy 10:18,19; 24:19; Joshua 24:14–24. Look at those passages again. Identify where they focus on what we believe and on how we should behave.

> **Think about...**
> On the Internet or in a large concordance, look up the words 'alien' and 'foreigner' and skim through the entire Bible. What overall pattern emerges? Many of the children we work with are not strictly speaking 'foreigners' for they are British. But in Bible times, these are the people of other faiths, many of whom were living amongst God's people.

during the period covered in the New Testament, where society was a mixture of Jew and Gentile, pagan, Arian, Greek. It was only when they lived in the desert or were establishing the kingdoms of Israel and Judah that they were a more monochrome society. But even then people of other faiths were always in the background of the stories we read. There is nothing new about our multicultural situation. We are living in a society that closely resembles that of much of Bible times, and particularly that of the New Testament.

You may have discovered by skimming through the Bible that there is far more discussion about how to *treat* foreigners than about what they *believe*. Of course, the people of Israel were told again and again not to get involved with idol worship or to worship anything or anyone other than God (Exodus 20:22–23; Joshua 24:14–24). To preserve the purity of their worship, God even ordered them to kill anyone who suggested worshipping other gods (Deuteronomy 13:10). These are difficult passages and need to be seen in their cultural context. Yet when the people of Israel found those of other faiths living near them, God wanted to equip them to relate to them.

Bible principles on relating to those of other faiths

These Biblical principles that urged people to relate to 'foreigners' are important for relating to people of other faiths today, whether adults or children.

Treat them with fairness and make sure they receive justice
(Leviticus 19:9–10,33–34; Zechariah 7:8–10)
When children of other faiths come to an event or club we are running, do we treat them fairly? Lots of people say, 'I treat them all the same', which often means we treat them all as white children. We don't ask the white children to act as Asian, but we might, unthinkingly perhaps,

ask the Asians to act white. For example we don't ask non-Muslims to wear headscarves but we might ask Muslim children to play a game that involves physical contact between boys and girls which may make many Muslims feel uncomfortable.

Love them
(Deuteronomy 10:18,19; Mark 12:31)
Easy to say but not so easy to do! These Bible verses may challenge prejudices. We may not be overtly racist, but we may make stereotypical assumptions about the Sikh lads we see driving round or Muslim women who are completely veiled. Do we love the asylum seekers who have moved into our area? How patient are we with the man

Think about…
Look at how people of other faiths are talked about in the media, or by people in your church. Are God's commands being obeyed? Think about the provision your church makes for children of other faiths compared with provision for children who are Christians or of no particular faith. Does this challenge you or your church?

In reality…
I once visited a very 'white' city with a group of Pakistani Muslims. As a white Christian, I experienced the negative reaction to our group – parents who moved their children away from us, people who laughed and pointed. To stand with those young people was a lesson for me in experiencing unfairness.

Top Tips: Welcoming children of other faiths   **7**

serving us in the shop who can hardly speak English? If we love someone then we are pleased to see them and spend time with them. Do we love people of other faiths living near us? How might we show this love to them?

Serve them unconditionally
(Matthew 25:31–46)

We don't know what happened to the people who are served in this story and we do not know whether they were or were not believers in Christ, but the emphasis is on whether people did or did not serve others in a Christlike way. Putting this parable in the context of the rest of the Gospel we have to conclude that just serving is not the way of salvation. But what this parable emphasises is that God wants his people to serve others regardless of whether the people being served make any sort of commitment to Jesus as a result – a reflection of Jesus' servant ministry. Jesus washed the disciples' feet, an act of total humility, and then commanded his disciples to follow his example of servanthood (John 13:1–17). His serving was not a means to an end, but an end in itself.

> **Think about…**
> Look at the following miracles and meetings: Luke 5:17–26; Luke 7:1–10,11–17; Luke 17:11–19; John 4:1–42. Then ask yourself these questions.
> - Whom did Jesus serve?
> - What did they ask of Jesus?
> - What did he do for them?
> - How did the person who was served respond?
> - How did the people who witnessed the miracle respond?

Jesus constantly served others without demanding a response, although, of course, there were occasions when he did challenge people to follow him. The results in the encounters above were dramatic. People's immediate needs were met (they were healed) and some went on to follow Jesus or to praise God, although we're not told whether they realised who Jesus was. The serving also had a wider impact on the people who witnessed what Jesus had done. Notice that his unconditional serving was extended to both Jews and non-Jews.

Working with children of other faiths is different to other children's work. Parents may be happy for their children to hear Bible stories and receive good, moral and God-centred teaching from Christians. But they may be strongly opposed to their children leaving their faith to become a Christian.

How do we balance our respect for the wishes of parents with our desire to see children meet Jesus in a personal way? Our ministry needs to be marked by a willingness to serve rather than by how many converts we can boast about. To measure 'success' by how far we have been able to follow Jesus' example of serving unconditionally can be liberating and refreshing. It is God who changes lives through our serving by the power of the Holy Spirit. This is the source of our hope!

In reality…

The leadership team of one holiday club that included many Muslim children spent a long time deciding how they would judge if they had been successful. In the end, their top success criteria were how far the team had served others and how far they had shown genuine love for the children and their families. Being freed from the pressure of counting the numbers who attended or who made a response helped the team understand their role, gave them confidence and reduced feelings of failure or guilt.

So the response the children make to Christ is ultimately up to them. This might seem a radical approach to children's work, but it reflects the way Jesus often worked, serving, caring and teaching but rarely pushing people to make declarations of faith or make the 'right' response although many obviously did become followers.

As with the woman of Samaria, people sometimes catch a glimpse of who Jesus really is through our words or our lives. At other times, we simply have to trust God to do his work in his way and time and never know what's gone on. The important thing is that regardless of response, Jesus continued to serve people.

You might say that it looks as though all we are doing is amateurish social work, without much Christian impact. But the following passages suggest a much more

Think about…

What are the needs of the children of other faiths in your community and around the neighbourhood of your church? Are you willing to keep on serving even though you don't see anyone becoming a Christian?

distinctive and radical motivation: Deuteronomy 10:17–22, Mark 12:30,31 and John 13:3–5. The love and care we have experienced from God is the basis for our serving. We don't serve because we are nice or because we feel guilty, but because we ourselves have been served. Our serving will be marked by a self-sacrificial love for the children that echoes God's love for us and for them (Deuteronomy 10:18).

> **In reality…**
> When we set up a holiday club for Muslim children we made sure that before parents booked for their children to come, they knew we were Christians and would be telling Bible stories. We were providing this 'service' because of our faith in Jesus.

What the Bible says about children in their community and family

To honour and obey their parents

There are many general instructions for all people which include children. But there is probably only one instruction directly for children: to honour and obey their parents (Exodus 20:12, Ephesians 6:1–3). Many children of other faiths come from cultures where respect for

family and respect for family authority has a far higher prominence than is the case for many western families. If a child wants to follow Jesus, helping them obey this command is probably one of the best things they can do.

Some people are called to be different and count the cost, but not all, all of the time
God doesn't ask everyone to stand up and be counted as Daniel had to. Daniel and his friends stood out from the crowd and faced fiery furnaces and lions' dens. But when the people of Israel were in exile, they were told to settle down, to seek the peace and prosperity of Babylon (Jeremiah 29:4–7). Esther and her uncle Mordecai bided their time. We must be careful not to place burdens on children to be different and count the cost, burdens that God is not giving them.

Or take the case of Naaman (2 Kings 5). Elisha seemed to understand Naaman's dilemma in serving his master. Naaman went to Elisha and asked for forgiveness for when, in the future, he would have to bow down to his master's god, Rimmon. Elisha's response was, "Go in peace!" (2 Kings 5:17–19). Sometimes it seems that faithfulness to God can best be lived out in quieter or more hidden ways, for the good of the individual and the wider community. But these circumstances will be relatively rare and probably only occur when we are a minority in a hostile environment.

> **Think about…**
> Look back at the passages we've considered.
> How might these influence your ministry with children of other faiths?
> How might they influence your relationship with God?
> What do you think God is saying to you and the wider church through them?

THE CHILDREN YOU MAY MEET

Believing, belonging, behaving!

For some years, churches have been challenged to identify what exactly defines someone as a member of a church. Is it by the way they live their lives, what they say and do, or the fact that they have chosen to belong or because they have agreed in their minds to a set of truths about Christ? Which comes first and are all three equally important and defining? This debate is relevant to our thinking here.

Adherents of other faiths may not express their belonging to a faith community in quite the same way as Christians do, emphasising practice as the way to identify which faith they belong to. For some it may be a badge of identity, 'I am a Muslim in name only' and nothing more. What makes

> **Think about…**
> Answer the following hypothetical quiz question.
> You are a Christian because you:
> a   Go to church on Sunday
> b   Celebrate Christmas and Easter
> c   Believe in the Lord Jesus Christ and have asked him to be your personal saviour.
> d   Have Christian parents
> e   Live in a Christian country
> You may have highlighted (c) as the key phrase since belief is essential to being a Christian and it is belief that influences actions. But is it that simple?

Top Tips: Welcoming children of other faiths

things more confusing is that even within one faith religious practices can vary from family to family. For example, Hindu families and communities do not worship the same representation of God.

In many faith communities belonging is corporate and therefore children often equate religion with the community of which they are part, expecting all people from that community to share the same faith. Research has shown that children seldom acknowledge that someone with the same mother tongue might be of a different faith community. They

> **In reality...**
> After being in school for a few weeks a Year 4 boy came to the head teacher in distress. In broken English he explained that he did not want to eat his dinner off a blue plate (which indicated he was not a vegetarian) because he wasn't a Christian. He assumed that it was only Christians who had blue plates. He had not associated the different colour of plates with types of food eaten but thought it indicated which religion you were.

need help in exploring how the experiences and values of particular cultures are worked out in different faith communities. For example Hindus, Sikhs, Muslims, Christians and others from the Indian subcontinent may all share the same cultural values of hospitality, respect for older people and consideration of the family's rather than the individual's interests. If children from this culture assume that Britain is a Christian country and therefore white British families are Christian, they may assume that the things they do are Christian. It is not surprising that certain aspects of British culture are understood as being accepted Christian practice. Ethnicity, culture and religion are being confused. Another way children identify themselves as belonging to a particular faith community is by contrasting their practice with those of other faiths. Children are very observant and recognise that these differences help to define the identity of their classmate. Whilst this can be very positive it is not always clear because the significance of religious identity varies. For example, recent research amongst children in mixed faith schools has highlighted that children from a white British family background are often regarded by others and

> **In reality...**
> In conversation about what food we like and don't like, Anaparma commented that she made tea differently to Christians. She assumed that it was Christian not to use spices but to put cold milk in first, followed by the tea infused hot water and sugar, whereas this is only a white English way of making tea. The Scots often put milk in after the tea! (Readers may choose to disagree!) To make spicy Masala tea like Anaparma why not visit www.recipedelights.com/recipes/beverages/masalatea.htm

> **Think about...**
> Look at the advertising hoardings in your local area. Could they be seen to represent a Christian lifestyle? What messages do they give?

themselves as Christian because they are not Muslim or Hindu or Sikh. In this instance Christian is a default term.

It is important for those who work with children who are educated and live in this rich diversity of cultures and faith groups to keep on listening and asking questions – so they can understand and be sensitive to the different ways children and adults identify themselves and others. They bring with them different experiences, practices and understanding.

It's not just faith...

English as an additional language

For many children English may not be their first language. So it is important to think about the words you use and concepts you are trying to explain. Build in fun ways to check that they understand words that are not in everyday use but perhaps part of the Bible stories you are sharing.

Consider opportunities to help children and their families develop their acquisition of the language by providing English classes for parents and extra lessons for the children. There are a wide range of courses on offer that would train you to teach English as a foreign language. Look in your local paper or local authority or college website to see what is available.

> **Think about...**
> Think of a child you know and brainstorm all the things that influence how they understand the world, how they react to peers and adults, what their hopes and dreams are. If you work with others share your thoughts and talk about how this affects the way you plan the things you do with the children you are meeting.

Asylum seekers and refugees
You may be working with children who have been granted refugee status or who are seeking asylum. They may be seeking asylum with both their parents or with only one parent or be separated from parents through the events that instigated their flight. They may be living with trauma resulting from what they have seen, heard or even experienced. Loss of a familiar environment is often compounded by being in a strange

> **In reality...**
> A mother, who had recently arrived in England, began to attend a parent and carer group with her baby where she soon felt a measure of acceptance. She then enrolled her 6-year-old son in the holiday club, where he needed continuous one-to-one support throughout the week. She was so grateful to the church because her son had such a wonderful week. He had begun his schooling in England at a special school because he could not speak and was very disruptive. But he had learned fast and was about to move into mainstream schooling. He had in fact, for the first five years of his life, never played outside and never played with other children because his parents lived in fear in their home country.

place, needing to learn a new language and being bewildered by the process of claiming refugee status.

You may find that the most important thing you can do in these early stages is to support the child and family in their everyday life:
- Explain how the school system works
- Provide appropriate equipment such as school bags, pencil cases, sports wear
- Support their acquisition of English
- Provide places of quiet such as homework clubs, or safe places to let off steam such as afterschool clubs
- Support the family by providing English classes for parents and help to complete official documents

The second/third generations

Not all migration is the result of asylum seeking. The UK has a rich history of people choosing to live and work here from all parts of the world. This has been encouraged and people from the Commonwealth and the European Union have moved to Britain to work, some for a short time whilst others settle down and make Britain their home. The children of these settlers who are born in the UK are often referred to as second

generation. They are usually fluent in both English and their mother tongue and become people who span two cultures. Films like *'Bend it like Beckham'* and *'East is East'* portray the lives of second generation Indians and the issues they face against a western cultural backdrop. These two different cultures can be in conflict and cause

confusion leaving the child neither one thing nor the other, but this is not always the case. Research has shown that many move easily from one situation to another, feeling at home in both and wanting to preserve elements of both cultures in their lives.

It is important therefore to recognise the different influences that are helping to shape these second and third generation children, the values that stem from the family and faith community and those that are learned at school, from the media and generally being part of British society.

3 PRACTICAL IDEAS

Getting started

Just asking how you might begin working with children of other faith backgrounds shows that you have already started. Already you may be spotting children and families who live in the next street or attend the same school as your children and wondering how you can get to know them. There is no set formula in getting started except perhaps that of prayer. But before praying about what you can do, spend some time researching your area to find out more about the families who live there. If you feel you are the only one in your  church who is interested in working with these children share what you have found out with your friends and church. You may be surprised that others have also caught the vision. Whether alone or with others make prayer for these particular families a priority.

> **Think about…**
> If you have access to the Internet check out your local authority website for census details of the people who live around your home or church. These are usually recorded according to electoral ward. List the different ways you and your church could serve those people.

Choose the best venue for your activity. If you want to run a cricket or football club then hiring the local community centre would probably be a better choice of venue than your church hall. Similarly if you were interested in setting up a homework club it may be possible to work with the school to provide a service, either in the school or elsewhere, that would fit into their extended schools provision. If you were running a church holiday club as

20 *Top Tips: Welcoming children of other faiths*

part of serving the community then the church hall would be the best place to hold this activity.

Working with the family

Children are part of families. Any work with children of other faiths must never lose sight of this fact. Everything we do must be open and welcoming to families as well as the children or young people themselves. Of course, families come in all shapes and sizes. One way to begin may be to set up a toddler group in your church and leaflet the local area inviting toddlers and their carers to attend. This could be the beginning of a relationship with not just the child but the whole family and lead to other opportunities like holiday clubs, homework clubs for older siblings and English classes or discussion groups for the parents.

> **In reality…**
> The ladies of a small church on a housing estate were aware that there was no place for the young teenagers to meet their friends. Most of the teenagers were Muslim. The ladies set up a weekly club for the girls in the community centre in the middle of the estate. Each week the girls took part in craft activities and discussion groups and enjoyed the space to sit and chat with friends.

Holiday clubs

One way of serving the community is to provide activities for school-aged children during the Easter or summer holidays or the half-term breaks of October and February. Both parents and children will welcome this.

Top Tips: Welcoming children of other faiths

Think carefully about the content of these sessions. Make sure that you are very open in what you do and say. You may want to post a timetable of the day's activities at the door of the hall so everyone is clear about what is happening. Why not invite parents to stay for coffee and a chat in a separate room or build in a session where children show the things they have learned and made? It is also useful to present the spiritual content of your club in a familiar format. All children experience school assemblies and therefore you may want to consider building on this model.

School assemblies

Schools with a large number of pupils from other faith families may have applied to the local SACRE body for a determination, which is an exemption from providing collective worship that is 'wholly or mainly of a broadly Christian character'. Whilst this means that most of their assemblies do not reflect the broad traditions of Christian belief it does not mean that none of them can. You may be one of a number of visitors to the school from different faith communities.

In reality…

Before I pray in a school assembly I share the following with the children:
'In a moment I am going to read a prayer. If you want to make this prayer your own, when I have finished, you can say "Amen" with me. That means that you agree. If you don't want to or can't for any reason, then that's fine. Just sit quietly with your own thoughts'.
Usually 'Amen' echoes across the room from most pupils but there are some who take advantage of this opportunity to opt out.

It is important to remember in the educational context of an assembly that the children have not chosen to be there. It is an opportunity to explain 'what the Bible says' or 'what Christians believe'. You may want to highlight both an application that Christians may draw from the assembly and an application that is relevant to all people whether they are Christians or not. This allows everyone the opportunity to take part and reflect on something that is relevant to their own life. Be guided by the school as to how they like to draw this time of reflection to a close. Many schools use guided silence with an agreed statement to signify the end of the time of reflection whilst others conclude with a prayer. It is important not to ask children to say, sing or pray things that they do not believe or that compromises their own faith.

Using stories

One of the best ways of explaining what Christians believe about God and the world is through the sharing of stories. All children love stories

and in particular love to be told stories. They may sometimes however find it a challenge to distinguish between fiction and real-life stories. You want them to know that the events of Jesus' birth, life, death and resurrection actually happened but that other stories, such as parables, contain important truths but are not accounts of actual events. When telling a story, try to differentiate between the truths contained in it and the historical events that occurred.

Someone once wrote that every story begins with 'and' and ends with 'and', because something happened before the story begins and something happens after it. This is true with the individual stories in the Bible. When you read or tell these individual stories you probably know what happened before or what will come next but the children may not. You may have the privilege of telling a story that has never been heard before by the children. Never underestimate the power of hearing a story for the first time!

Of course, as the storyteller, you are part of the faith community that recognises that these Bible stories reveal something about the God you serve. The children you are sharing these stories with are probably not and therefore cannot see the stories with the eyes of a believer. This will affect how they understand them.

As you plan a storytelling session examine it yourself first, asking these questions:
- What does this story tell me about God?
- What does it tell me about the world God has made?
- How do the characters relate to God and to each other?
- What does that tell me about how I should relate to God?

You might want to note down your reflections and think about which ones you want to focus on and how you can draw these ideas out of the story. Then practise how you will begin your story and tell the middle part and the end. Prepare whatever storytelling techniques you are going to use too. Whatever you do, don't mess up a storytelling opportunity for lack of preparation!

Don't forget that the children who listen also bring to the story their own ideas about God, the world and where they fit into it. Their ideas may be similar to yours or quite different. One way to find this out is to build in questions as you tell the story:
- What do you think he said or did?
- How do you think they felt when this or that happened?

> **In reality...**
> I was recounting the story of Solomon who had to make the difficult decision as to who was the real mother of a baby claimed by two mothers as theirs. I had reached the part where he had decided to cut the baby in half. I described how he raised his arm with his sword held high. A great intake of breath was heard across the room as the children realised the implications of his actions and waited for the dreaded deed to take place. Why? They had never heard the story before and were mightily relieved when the real mother spoke out.

25

Top Tips: Welcoming children of other faiths

> **In reality…**
> During the story of the twelve spies I reached the point where ten of them told Moses it was too dangerous to go on, whereas Joshua and Caleb argued that God had told them to go, so that's what they should do. I asked the listening children from many different faith backgrounds, 'Who did the people listen to, the ten or the two?' They all said the two because God had said to go. When I told them that in actual fact the people listened to the ten they were really stunned because the people had clearly disobeyed God.

You will probably be amazed at the insights the children have!

Everyone who tells Bible stories to children knows their power. It can be as if time is suspended as the tale unfolds and everyone, storyteller and audience alike, is carried along right to the end. Undoubtedly God is present at such an occasion and is working in those present. Sometimes it is obvious, but not always and it's in those times that we need to trust that God is making himself known.

In talking to Nicodemus, Jesus told him, "The wind blows wherever it pleases. You hear its sound, but you cannot tell where it comes from or where it is going". So it is with us. The Holy Spirit may be doing something very powerful with his Word in the lives of those listening to it.

Using songs

When choosing songs to use with children from other faith backgrounds avoid songs that are confessional (that is, ones that require the singer to be committed to God to be sung with any meaning). Instead, look for songs that declare

something of the nature of God. Many of the scriptural songs do just that. Check out www.scriptureunion.org.uk/music for Learn and Remember music tracks. If you are working with children over a long period of time you may choose to begin with simple songs of declaration and only later introduce songs that contain profound Christian doctrine (for example *Light for Everyone* from the CD of the same name which although not confessional does require a deeper understanding of the Christian faith).

Using Scripture

All children have good memories and you may want to build in opportunities for remembering Bible verses when running Christian clubs at school or at church. If you are using memory verses in your sessions, think carefully about the verses you choose, why you have chosen those particular verses and which version of the Bible you are using. This might be the first time the children have come across a verse so think about whether they understand the words or if you need to unpack it. Again choose verses that explain who God is or give wisdom for living, avoiding verses that are confessional or

> **Think about…**
> List a few of the songs you sang as a child or sing today with the children you work with. Think about the words contained in those songs and make two columns headed Confession and Declaration. Which songs would go where?

> **In reality…**
> One experienced schools worker thinks carefully about the songs he uses. If he wants to use a confessional song then he explains to the children he is going to sing a special song to God and invites them to listen.

confrontational. You may want to combine memory verses with music and there are lots of fun songs that do just that.

Think about where in your programme this would come as you may want to give children the option of not learning these verses. It is, however, good practice to provide copies for them to take home and share with their families.

> **In reality…**
>
> The children who attended our children's club were mainly from the Gujarati community and they loved singing Scripture songs. One of their favourites was 'He's a Rock' by John Hardwick and after singing the words 'Look up chapter 32 verse 4 of Deuteronomy' they did just that and were amazed that the words they were singing were there in the Bible.

TEN TOP TIPS FOR WORKING WITH CHILDREN OF OTHER FAITHS

Do...

- respect the faith and culture of the children.
- use music, artwork and methods that are culturally appropriate.
- be open and honest in the presentation of the Christian faith.
- be open and honest about the content of what you are doing with parents and other adults involved in their lives.
- seek to build long-term friendships that are genuine and not dependent upon conversion.

Don't...

- assume they understand what you mean when you say you are a Christian.
- criticise, ridicule or belittle other religions or cultures.
- tell the children what their faith says or define it by what some of its adherents do.
- ask children to say, sing or pray things that they do not believe or that compromise their own faith.
- encourage them to make decisions that would put them in conflict with their family.

GLOSSARY

Mother tongue
Collins Dictionary definition is 'One's native language'. It usually refers to the language of the community and is often the first language spoken by the child.

Bend it like Beckham
British comedy film by Gurinder Chadha in 2002. The film explores the issues surrounding two girls, one white British, the other Asian British, who take up football in the face of parental disapproval. Certificate 12.

East is East
British comedy film by Ayub Khan-Din in 1999. The film is about a family growing up in Britain in the 1970s. The father is Pakistani and the mother white British. Some of the issues raised are those of identity, family honour and living in two cultures. Certificate 15.

Asylum seeker
An asylum seeker is someone who is awaiting a Home Office decision as to whether they can remain in the UK.

Refugee
The 1951 convention relating to the status of refugees defined a refugee as being a person who, owing to a well founded fear of being persecuted for reasons of race, religion, nationality, membership in a particular group, or political opinion, is outside the country of his nationality, and is unable to, or, owing to such fear, is unwilling to avail himself of the protection of that country.

Ethnicity
Identity with or participation in a particular racial group.

Culture
In this context culture means a community's overall way of life. This includes the ideas, beliefs, attitudes as well as actions, which the group considers important and which it holds in common as a group. (Taken from NACCCE report *All our futures* p41.)

SACRE
Standing Advisory Council on Religious Education. All local authorities have a SACRE which is a permanent body that advises on all aspects of the provision of RE and collective worship in schools.

Useful resources

Anyone can tell a story Bob Hartman (Lion Hudson)
(An inspiring and easy read that will affect your storytelling forever!)

The Bible and Other Faiths: what does the Lord Require of Us? Ida Glaser (IVP).
(One of the most helpful books on what the Bible says about other faiths.)

Children's perspectives on believing and belonging – This University of East London report is on the Joseph Rowntree site:
www.jrf.org.uk/knowledge/findings/socialpolicy/0375

Sarah Mayers was the commissioning editor who created and developed the Top Tip series of booklets. The vision behind the series was driven by her passion to reach children and young people with the good news of Jesus. She wanted to equip children's and youth workers to be as effective as possible.

This was the last book that she edited before her death in December 2006. We are grateful to God for her life and ministry, aware that the impact of the books she wrote and edited will be felt for many years to come.